A Life of
Devotion

52 Weekly Reflection to Guide You
Towards a Life of Faith and Peace

Betty Gossell

Riverview Press

A Life of Devotion
Copyright © 2022 by Betty Gossell

ISBN: (Paperback)   979-8986772561
       (eBook)   979-8986772578

The view expressed in this book are solely those of the author and do not necessarily reflect the views of the publisher, and the publisher hereby disclaims any responsibility for them.

Riverview Press

CONTENTS

DEDICATION

Both of my parents have passed away from this earthly world and moved on to their heavenly rewards – my dad in July of 2015 and my mom in February 2022. But the impact they made on my life will continue for generations.

When I was born, we lived on a tiny farm in northern Minnesota. Our four-room house had no running water and was pretty crowded. My mother was a nurse at the local hospital and my dad worked in a factory in addition to running the farm. It was a very difficult life, I'm sure. We moved to a town in northern Iowa when I was a few months old. One of my earliest memories was going to church as a family, the seven of us filling up most of a pew. Teaching, giving to others, serving on committees, and taking leadership roles – all these things were demonstrated for us regularly. We ate our meals together as a family each evening and we took turns saying the prayer. They modeled for us hard work, ethics, and integrity. Most of the devotions in this book are taken from lessons they taught me over the years. Others are things I went on to learn later in life, but still reflect the values and principles I was taught as a child. My hope is that I have been able to pass many of these qualities on to my daughter and then to her daughter as well.

Of course, there have been many others who have had great influence on me over the years – pastors from various churches, teachers, special friends, and neighbors. But there has been no greater influence than my parents Ed and Wanda. This book is dedicated to them, and to all the other loving parents who do their best each day to 'train up a child in the way he should go; and when he is old, he will not depart from it.'

Betty Gossell

INTRODUCTION

Finding time for Bible study is not always easy with the hectic lives we all live. I know I always have good intentions at the start of a new year, but before a few weeks go by I miss a day here and a day there, and then I feel like it's too hard to get caught up.

The format of these devotionals is very simple – they are structured so that you do one per week. Each will take less than 15 minutes to complete. Of course, if you miss a week, just jump back in wherever you want. The devotions include a scripture, a short reflection, a prayer and then there is room to leave your thoughts.

Additionally, they do not have to be read in any special order – if you are dealing with a particular struggle, feel free to skip ahead to which ever reading would be the most beneficial.

My prayer is that you find these reflections to be helpful and that they spur some introspection. I can only hope they bless you as much to read as they did me to write.

Betty Gossell

WEEK 1 – NEW CREATURE

Today's Scripture: II Corinthians 5:17 "Therefore, if anyone is in Christ, the new creation has come: The old has gone, the new is here!"

Reflection: The start of a new year causes many people to think about New Year's Resolutions. Whether it is to lose weight, get in shape, save money, or develop better habits like making their bed every day, the new calendar offers endless possibilities and 12 months of blank spaces to fill. The question is, what will we fill them with?

Today's verse tells us that if we are in Christ, we are a new creature. But what does a new creature need to survive and thrive? Thinking of an infant, we know they need food, water, shelter, and someone to care for them and teach them the skills they need to learn to succeed in the world. As Christians, we are much the same. We need daily nourishment from scripture, the shelter of faith that comes from a vibrant relationship with

Jesus, and the care and instruction from others to help us navigate this troubled society. What if we made it our resolution this year to cherish our new creature and fill our lives with God's word, God's presence, and God's people?

Prayer: Dear Heavenly Father, thank you for this new year and all the opportunities it brings. Thank you for the blessings you so willingly bestow on us. Help us to rely on you for the nourishment of your word, strength in our relationship with you, and instruction from (and fellowship with) other believers. Amen

Application:

_____

_____

_____

_____

_____

_____

WEEK 2 – SNOWSTORM

Today's Scripture: Psalm 78:52 "But he led his own people like a flock of sheep, guiding them safely through the wilderness."

Reflection: The farm where I lived as a child had a really long driveway, or at least it seemed long to me as a little girl. When I was in kindergarten, I rode a bus to the school that was a few miles away. One day, it started snowing very heavily and we were sent home early. The snow was so intense and the winds so strong, you could not see many of the homes from the road! Our elementary principal Mr. K rode the bus with us and walked each of us to our door, so he was sure we got into our homes safely. When the bus got to my farm, I was pretty scared. Mr. K took my hand, and we started walking toward my house which was invisible in the snow. He told me that the school had called my dad and that he would be looking for us. Mr. K held my hand tightly as we walked through the blizzard, and I started to feel safe, and also, I felt important to him, knowing that he would take the time to walk me home. He was patient as my tiny legs struggled through the deepening snow. About halfway to the house, I heard my dad walking toward us. I could not see him yet, but I heard his voice. Finally, I was able to make out his features and was so relieved! He thanked Mr. K for walking me home, who then turned to go back to the bus that was waiting on the side of the road. There were several other children he was responsible for as well. Dad held my hand as we walked the rest of the way to the house where he helped me get out of my wet clothes and boots.

As I read today's verse, I was reminded of this incident from so many years ago. The wilderness I experienced was a blizzard of howling winds and a wall of heavy snow that obscured my view. Without Mr. K's guidance, who knows where I would have wandered and if I would have even found my house. How much more does our heavenly father want to guide us if we but let him. Even when we are afraid and unable to see the path before us, we can trust that he will lead us safely home.

Prayer: Dear Father – thank you for your guidance during the difficult times of my life. Help me to reach out and take your hand, and to not be afraid. You can see the road ahead, even when I cannot. Thank you for the love you show each day to lead me in paths of safety. Amen

Application:

_____

_____

_____

_____

_____

_____

WEEK 3 – THINK ON THESE THINGS

Today's Scripture: Philippians 4:8 "Finally, brethren, whatsoever things are true, whatsoever things are honest, whatsoever things are just, whatsoever things are pure, whatsoever things are lovely, whatsoever things are of good report; if there be any virtue, and if there be any praise, think on these things."

Reflection: What types of things do we fill our minds with each day? What TV shows, YouTube videos, music or audio books do we listen to? What conversations do we participate in? What do we say to ourselves when we are all alone?

When I was a little girl living on a farm in Iowa, we always had a barn full of cats to help chase the mice and keep us kids entertained. I loved cats, especially my black and white cat Spotty. He was a great cat who loved to cuddle and play. He was eternally patient when I dressed him in doll clothes and pushed him around in a buggy, but one day something scared him, and he managed to leave me with a huge deep scratch that went from my elbow to my wrist. My mother washed it and applied antibiotic ointment, but I continued to cry and complain about how much it hurt. She finally asked me more about the pain, and I said, "When I look at it, it hurts!" "So, don't look at it!" she replied. Her answer surprised me a bit, but I soon realized that when I stopped thinking about it and staring at it, it did not hurt so badly. Instead, I was able to focus on other things and go back to playing without crying or pain.

It is the same now that we are adults. Filling our minds with violent images or inappropriate language, participating in conversations involving gossip, or dwelling on negative circumstances beyond our control will limit the beautiful things that God wants to fill us with instead.

Prayer: Lord, help us to remember to focus our thoughts on you and the blessings you have given us. You created this amazing planet and all the plants and animals who live here. You loved us enough to send your Son to save us from an eternity separated from you. You want to fill our lives with joy and peace. Help us to think on these things. Amen

Application:

_____

_____

_____

_____

_____

_____

WEEK 4 – NEEDY

Today's Scripture: Proverbs 31:20 "She opens her arms to the poor and extends her hands to the needy."

Reflection: One of my favorite books when I was growing up was Little Women. It is the story of the March family – four young daughters and their mother who were left to fend for themselves while their father was fighting in the Civil War. They were quite poor, and the book begins with the girls longing for Christmas presents but knowing there was no money. On Christmas morning they awoke to find a meager breakfast and a small gift or two. As they were about to start eating, Mother walked in with news of a nearby family with a new baby, no wood for heat and no food. The baby was sick, and the other children were starving. The girls quickly packed up their sparse breakfast, loaded their arms with some precious firewood, and headed out to spread Christmas cheer. As hard as it was for them to give up their simple breakfast, they used it as a blessing for others.

How willing are we to share with others, especially if we feel we are struggling ourselves? Whether we fear that the gift will seem inadequate, or are worried about meeting our own needs first, the temptation is to feel like we need to wait until we can do something big before reaching out to others. What we often fail to realize is that our meager gift could mean the world to someone else. God sees our offerings and is faithful to reward us later.

Footnote: The March sisters returned home to find an elaborate Christmas lunch that was given to them by a wealthy neighbor after he had heard of their generosity. In the same way, God will pour out blessings we cannot imagine if we will but obey him and share what we have (even if it is all we have) with those who are in need.

Prayer: Dear Father, help us to see the needs in the world around us, and to respond by sharing the gifts you have so lavishly given us. Even in times of difficulty, we can share care and compassion to others. Thank you for loving us and for providing for our needs. Amen

Application:

_____

_____

_____

_____

_____

_____

WEEK 5 – IMITATION

Today's Scripture: Ephesians 5:1 "Therefore be imitators of God, as beloved children."

Reflection: My dad loved to go duck hunting. He and a friend from his work spent numerous hours turning an old boat into a duck blind and they loved to sit on the water with his hunting dog Duchess. With duck calls in hand and decoys floating nearby, they waited patiently for the flocks to come within range. One year my dad decided he wanted to hunt Canadian geese as well but did not have any geese decoys. I remember sitting with him in his shop while he cut white Styrofoam blocks into various pieces and glued them together to resemble geese of different shapes and sizes. He used a knife to whittle their heads to look as accurate as possible, and then I helped him with the painting. He showed me pictures from a book so I would know what they were to look like. He was so excited to take them hunting the next weekend, and he and his buddy came home with a trunk full of geese. The decoys were so realistic that the real geese could not tell the difference and glided down onto the water beside them. Dad's imitations were an accurate reflection of the real thing.

Our verse today tells us we are to be imitators of God. But what does that mean, and how do we accomplish it? First off, we need a picture of what we are to look like, and there is no better guide for us than God's word. But we also need the skilled hands of someone who molds and shapes us into accurate representations of Jesus. Through prayer and instruction from others, we will grow in our likeness of God.

Prayer: Dear God, what I want more than anything is to be like you – to look like you, act like you, and speak like you in this troubled world. Help me to not be afraid to have the excess carved away, but to willingly open my heart to become more like you every day. And may my imitation be such that others are drawn to you. Amen

Application:

_____

_____

_____

_____

_____

_____

WEEK 6 – JENNY

Today's Scripture: Ephesians 1:13 "I pray that the eyes of your heart may be enlightened in order that you may know the hope to which he has called you, the riches of his glorious inheritance in his holy people,"

Reflection: My father's cousin Jenny was an accomplished painter whose artwork was well-received in the local community. She also played piano at church and had a quiet, beautifully caring spirit. When she was in her 40's she started losing her eyesight and doctors were unable to help her. Before long, she was totally blind and forced to put her paint brushes away. For about 20 years she was in complete darkness, but amazingly was able to continue playing piano. She lived with her sister who provided total care for her. But her faith in God never wavered, despite the loss of her artistic dreams. One day an eye surgeon approached her with an experimental procedure that he hoped would restore partial vision in one of her eyes. He felt this was her last chance – if this failed, he had nothing further to offer her. "I trust God, whatever happens," she told him as she was wheeled into the operating room. Much to everyone's delight, 80% vision was restored in her left eye! She could see again! Sunrises, the changes in her surroundings and even her own reflection in the mirror – she could see it all! The very first thing she did was pick up a paintbrush and soon she was painting beautiful pictures for each of us in the family.

Just as Jenny's physical eyesight was restored, God wants the eyes of our hearts to be open to all the wonderful things he does for us. He doesn't want us walking around blind to the beauty of this world or to the hope of an eternity spent with him in heaven. Take time each day to thank him for all his provisions to you: both in the past and in the future as well.

Prayer: Open my eyes, Lord, to all the wonderful things you do for me and how your provision is all I need. Thank you for your love, and for the hope of heaven and an eternity with you. Amen

Application:

_____

_____

_____

_____

_____

_____

WEEK 7 – HOLY

Today's Scripture: Revelation 4:8 "Holy, holy, holy, Lord God Almighty, which was, and is, and is to come."

Reflection: When my family attended our small country church, we occupied an entire pew. As one of the younger children, I would often sit at one end of the row with dad and my baby brother was at the other end with mom. My three older siblings would be somewhere in the middle. It was the early 1960's, and we were always scrubbed clean and wearing our 'Sunday Best.' I remember standing on the pew next to my dad and learning to read as his fingers pointed out the words from our well-worn red hymnal. One particular favorite was 'Holy, Holy, Holy.' I was too young to know what cherubims or seraphims were, but as I listened to the singing, I was able to catch a glimpse of God's majesty and power. There were other songs, of course, that taught me about the Love of God and that there was Power in the Blood, but this one stands out to me. It

—

taught me that God WAS, as we learned about in the Old Testament with stories of Moses, Noah, and David. I learned that God IS – he was part of the world around me now and I could talk to him as both my creator and my friend. And then there was the phrase about him being God of WHAT IS TO COME. I didn't need to worry about the future – God was already there, working out what was best for me if I would just trust him. Past, present, and future: God is Lord of it all.

Prayer: Dear Heavenly Father – thank you for loving us then, and for loving us now. Thank you for the old hymns which taught us Biblical lessons before we were old enough to understand, or even read on our own.

Holy, holy, holy! All the saints adore thee, Casting down their golden crowns around the glassy sea. Cherubim and seraphim falling down before thee, Which wert, and art, and evermore shalt be. Amen

Application:

_____

_____

_____

_____

_____

_____

WEEK 8 – HARMONY

Today's Scripture: Colossians 3:14 "And above all these put on love, which binds everything together in perfect harmony."

Reflection: Whether listening to a string quartet at a wedding or to a 100-piece symphony at a large music hall, the exquisite harmonies of professional musicians is a rare treat. High or low, soft or loud, fast or slow – each member has a specific part to play. But have you ever thought about what it takes to blend the multiple instruments into a magical experience? The performers have spent hours and hours in practice for decades, both individually and as a group, long before you ever took your seat in the auditorium. The squeaky notes when they first picked up an instrument as a child; the hours spent in lessons both at school and at home; listening to their directors as they learned to hone their craft – all of these are brought together on this special occasion. We cannot judge the strength of the relationship based solely on what we see in public, without knowing the sacrifices that went on in private.

Today's verse talks about love bringing perfect harmony. But it usually doesn't start out that way. There will be rocky beginnings in any relationship, and at various times throughout the relationship as well. It takes lots of practice and teamwork to develop genuine love. Only with God as our conductor will that love become perfect. Sometimes you need to play quietly in a supportive role while others take the lead. Other times it will be your turn to step up into a more prominent place in the relationship. But in every case, we need to trust the conductor who knows how to bring out the best performance from each member.

Prayer: Dear Father, help us to remember that you are the ultimate conductor of our lives. You know what is best for each of us, and for the world as a whole. Help us to learn to listen to your guidance, and to work to blend our lives together with you into perfect harmony and love. Amen

Application:

_____

_____

_____

_____

_____

_____

WEEK 9 – MAPS

Today's Scripture: Isaiah 58:11 "The LORD will guide you always; he will satisfy your needs in a sun-scorched land and will strengthen your frame."

Reflection: I have always loved maps and globes and learning about geography. From a very early age, I remember sitting next to my dad in the car and looking at the folded maps he kept in the glove box to figure out where we were and how far we were from our destination. He taught me directions, what the different colors and symbols on the maps meant, and the ever-important skill of how to refold the map when I was done! He also taught me to read highway signs and the importance of mile markers. And many years later I taught those skills to my daughter as well.

I recall one particular trip when my family was on vacation and driving across Nebraska during the hottest week on record. Our car had air conditioning, but dad didn't like to turn it on. All seven of us in the car were suffering in the heat and cramped quarters. Finally, he gave in to our pleadings and agreed to stop at the next town for ice cream and cold drinks. He had me find the nearest town on the map and we counted down the miles until we could get out of the crowded car, stretch our legs, and cool off.

God works in much the same way. When we are hot and tired, He guides us to places of His refreshment. When we are lost and don't know where to turn, He teaches us to recognize the signs around us that point us in the direction we should go. And like my earthly father, He patiently teaches skills that will help us guide others in the future.

Prayer: Dear Heavenly Father – thank you for guiding us when we are unsure where to go, and for leading us to quiet streams of renewal. Thank you also for providing signs that point us toward you. Thank you for being our ever-present help when we need you. Amen

Application:

_____

_____

_____

_____

_____

_____

WEEK 10 – GOD OF POWER

Today's Scripture: Ephesians 1:19-21 "I also pray that you will understand the incredible greatness of God's power for us who believe him. This is the same mighty power that raised Christ from the dead and seated him in the place of honor at God's right hand in the heavenly realms. Now he is far above any ruler or authority or power or leader or anything else—not only in this world but also in the world to come."

Reflection: Have you ever really stopped to think about the immense power that was necessary for God to bring Jesus back to life? After being beaten, bruised and crucified, He was placed in a tomb for three days. His body was denied food and water, his heart was not beating, his brain and vital organs were starved of blood and oxygen. Rigor mortis had certainly set in. But at the appropriate time, with one burst of power from God's hand, Jesus was brought back to life!

I imagine it like a giant defibrillator! His heart started beating, blood was pumping, oxygen began flowing, muscles were moving, and all of his senses and body systems were restored. Leaving the grave clothes behind, he WALKED out of the tomb totally healthy and healed! But as amazing as that is to fathom, Paul tells us in our scripture that we as believers have access to that same power! We are not to feel helpless when life's trials surround us. We are not to feel defeated when others treat us badly. As children of the King, we are to feel confident and powerful as we confront the daily challenges of this world. Just as God restored life and breath within Jesus, we can be filled with that same power to help restore life and love to those around us.

Prayer: Oh Lord of Power and Might, we stand in awe at Your amazing strength. We marvel at Your creation of the universe and all within it. We cannot comprehend all that You have accomplished, including raising Jesus from the dead. Thank you for loving us and providing all we need to face the challenges of the world around us. Amen

Application:

_____

_____

_____

_____

_____

_____

WEEK 11 – ENCOURAGE

Today's Scripture: Romans 1:11-12 "I long to see you so that I may impart to you some spiritual gift to make you strong— that is, that you and I may be mutually encouraged by each other's faith."

Reflection: I remember the first time I walked into our local public library. It was a very old building, probably 100 years old, with multiple floors and a circular staircase. Throughout my childhood and teen years, I went there quite often to check out books to read for fun or to research term papers for school. The woodwork was dark and massive, and I was enthralled by the number of books that were stacked to the ceiling, sometimes in little hidden alcoves and covered in dust. Each book I checked out felt like a special gift saved just for me. Whether a Nancy Drew mystery or an Encyclopedia Britannica, each held the promise of a new adventure or world to explore. As a child, my mother took me every two weeks during the summer, and I couldn't wait for my chance to wander and explore and find new treasures.

Do we feel the same excitement about spending time with our Christian friends, learning from each other and sharing our faith? Do we have words of wisdom and encouragement to offer each other? What gifts do we give? Our time? Our compassion? Our listening ear and caring heart? What words do we offer? Those of some best-selling crime author, or those of the author and finisher of our faith?

Prayer: Dear Heavenly Father – thank you for friends who are willing to share encouragement and words of wisdom when we need them. Help us to reach out to others and to see times when we need to share our faith. Each of us has times of weakness and times of strength. Help us to be willing to share both. Amen

Application:

_____

_____

_____

_____

_____

_____

WEEK 12 – GOLD

Today's Scripture: Proverbs 8:19 "My fruit is better than gold and precious stones, and my increase more worth than fine silver."

Reflection: One of our family vacations took us to South Dakota where we had the opportunity to pan for gold. Each of us was given a small pie pan and we stood along a cold river sifting and rinsing the dirt while looking for pieces of gold. All of us dreamed of being lucky and finding something of value. After several minutes I got excited when I saw flashes of light and flecks of gold at the bottom of one of my pans. I was going to be rich! But it turned out to be Fool's Gold, iron pyrite. Unlike the real thing, Fool's Gold is a relatively worthless commodity because of its natural abundance and lack of industrial use. I still thought it was pretty and brought it home in a sandwich bag. It was just enough to fill a small baby food jar. Even though it was shiny, the fruit of my labors was a cup of disappointment. But

I kept it as a reminder to continue to search for the truth.

God wants the fruits of our lives to be pure gold, not worthless Fool's Gold. We are to produce things that are of value, highly prized and sought after, and not be satisfied to be worthless jars on the shelf.

Prayer: Dear Father, I want the fruits of my life to be genuine and pure, not cheap imitations of your plan for me. And although others in my life may distract me by their flashy temptations, help me keep my focus on you and your pure love for me. Amen

Application:

_____

_____

_____

_____

_____

_____

WEEK 13 – STREETLIGHTS

Today's Scripture: Psalm 19:1-2 "The heavens declare the glory of God; the skies proclaim the work of his hands. Day after day they pour forth speech; night after night they reveal knowledge."

Reflection: In the summer of 2000, I was working in Tucson, AZ, as a consultant at one of the hospitals. It took me a few days to realize that the streetlights seemed a bit dim, and it was darker than usual while I was driving around after sunset. I asked one of my coworkers about this and she explained that the streetlights were less bright on purpose so as not to interfere with the astronomy observatories on the nearby mountains. One evening we took a drive to just outside the city limits and I was in awe of the beauty of the night sky. Never before had I see the stars and constellations so clearly, and the Milky Way seemed so close that I could almost touch it. My friend explained that by reducing the illumination from the streetlights by even a small percentage, it made a huge difference in what could be seen by both the naked eye and at the research observatories.

It caused me to think about my own life – what good things do I have (my job, caring for my family and my home, doing charity work) that are actually interfering with what God wants to bless me with? Streetlights are a good thing, guiding and protecting us while we drive at night. But Tucson was able to find a balance between safety and the beauty of the stars. Maybe I need to 'dim the lights' a bit on my busyness – whether it is housework or on my computer - and spend time learning what God wants to show me.

Prayer: Lord, help me to find balance in my life. Work, home, school, family – all of these are good things. But sometimes I get so busy with these 'things' that I neglect to sit quietly and see the beauty around me, and to learn more about what you desire for my life. I want to see you more clearly, even if it means dimming the lights elsewhere. Amen

Application:

_____

_____

_____

_____

_____

_____

WEEK 14 – A MOTHER'S LOVE

Today's Scripture: Proverbs 31:26-27 "She opens her mouth with wisdom, and loving instruction is on her tongue. She watches over the ways of her household and does not eat the bread of idleness."

Reflection: Learning is not always done in a formal setting, and children will model our behavior as much or more as our instructions. My mother never slept late, even on weekends or holidays. She cooked three meals each day for our large family, back in the time before microwaves or packaged foods. She had no dishwasher, and drive throughs had not been invented. She was always cooking, cleaning, or doing laundry (and ironing!) our mountains of clothes. She refinished and reupholstered furniture and took excellent care of the few 'things' we did own. I remember on Saturday nights she would make sure each of us children had a bath and our church clothes (many that she had sewn herself) were ready for the next day. After we all went to bed, she would polish our church shoes and sit them out on the kitchen counter to dry. Very little was ever thrown away – she was always looking for ways to reuse or repurpose items for us or for others. She did teach me to sew and bake, hobbies I enjoyed into adulthood. But the biggest lessons I learned from her were about devotion to family, completing a job once you start it, and still finding time to care for others.

Prayer: Lord, thank you for mothers who provide Godly examples for us – hard work, stewardship of the earth, and faithfulness to our families. Help me to be that type of example to my child and grandchild. Amen

Application:

_____

_____

_____

_____

_____

_____

WEEK 15 – GIFTS

Today's Scripture: I Peter 4:10 "Each of you should use whatever gift you have received to serve others, as faithful stewards of God's grace in its various forms."

Reflection: It's easy to feel as if we don't have any real gifts, or the gifts we have are small and insignificant. Perhaps we are not in a leadership role at our place of worship, or maybe we sing in the choir but do little else. It's hard not to feel inferior to those who have more or bigger gifts than we do. But God has given all of us gifts, and it's our responsibility to recognize them, develop them as best we can, and find ways to use them.

Many years ago, I was in my early 20's and living more than 1000 miles away from my family. As exciting as it was to be on my own, it was also a struggle financially and emotionally. I had an old car that my dad had given me, but it was a constant source of frustration with many needed repairs. I just didn't have the finances to fix everything and was quite concerned. One day, one of the men from the church that I was attending reached out to me and offered to look at my car for me. He ran a local repair shop and although I trusted him to give me an honest assessment of my car, I was secretly very worried about how much everything was going to cost. Imagine my surprise when he returned my car to me (now in perfect running order) and said there would be no charge! I cried when he handed my keys back to me – I don't think he had any idea how much his kindness meant to me that day. He used his gifts in auto repair to bless me in ways he could never imagine. I will never forget his kindness.

Prayer: Dear Heavenly Father – help us to recognize the gifts you have given to each of us. Whether we are up front leading worship or working behind the scenes in a supportive role, you have given each of us talents and gifts, and a job to do. Open my eyes to avenues of service that are all around me and help me to step out in boldness to walk through the doors you open for me. Amen

Application:

_____

_____

_____

_____

_____

_____

WEEK 16 – FEAR

Today's Scripture: Psalm 34:4 "I sought the Lord, and he answered me and delivered me from all my fears."

Reflection: Trembling with fear, I stood beside my parents' bed, afraid to wake them up but in need of comfort. I was quite young, maybe four or five years old, but had been having bad dreams and dreaded falling asleep again. Finally, I tapped my mother on her arm and she groggily opened her eyes. One look at the tears streaming down my cheeks was all she needed before she pulled back the covers and let me slip into bed between her and dad. Whispering softly (so as not to wake dad) she asked me what the trouble was. I told her I had a scary dream with a bad guy who was chasing me. She pulled me close and stroked my hair. "Well, there are no bad guys here. Do you think you can get back to sleep?" I curled up next to her and was enveloped by the smell of her perfume and the softness of her silky nightgown. Soon I was resting peacefully.

Dear friend, don't you know that God is just waiting for us to bring our fears to him? We don't need to be afraid to wake him because he never sleeps. He is always watching out for us, wanting what is best. He desires to take us into his arms, to brush away our tears, and to help us rest in the assurance of his love.

Prayer: Dear Father, sometimes I am so afraid and worried about things that are out of my control. Please help me to remember to run to you, to crawl up in your lap and let your arms of strength and comfort wrap around me. Your love is the answer to my fears. Amen

Application:

_____

_____

_____

_____

_____

_____

WEEK 17 – PRIDE AND JOY

Today's Scripture: 3 John 1:4 "I have no greater joy than to hear that my children are walking in the truth."

Reflection: My older brother was very involved in sports when we were in high school. All four years he played varsity football, wrestled, ran track, and played baseball. Dad especially loved to watch him play football, and even got his only speeding ticket rushing to a game one Friday night after work. There was never a second thought about traveling to his away games, even if the weather was bad. In fact, his last football game was played in below-freezing temperatures with sleet covering the metal bleachers. Long car rides to tournaments, entire Saturdays spend in the gym watching wrestling matches, endless hours in the sun at baseball games – despite it all, nothing made my dad happier than to watch his oldest son do his best playing sports.

Our verse today talks about an earthly joy that is felt when young converts are following God. But I could not help but think how much more our heavenly father feels joy when we turn our lives over to him, when we seek him daily (even if the weather is bad or the days are long) and keep doing our best day after day, year after year.

Prayer: Dear Father, at the end of the day, what matters most is that my actions and words have brought you joy. Help me to not grow weary when the days are long or I'm uncomfortable in my surroundings. All I want is to honor you. Amen

Application:

_____
_____
_____
_____
_____
_____

WEEK 18 – HEAR MY VOICE

Today's Scripture: John 10:14 "I am the good shepherd; I know my own sheep, and they know me."

Reflection: My life as a small child, growing up on a farm was a life full of adventure and surprises. Too young to be responsible for many chores, my days were filled with fun. There were lots of animals to play with, trees to climb, and a creek to explore – what more could a little girl want? But few days were more exciting than when my dad brought home a newborn lamb for us to care for. The mother had delivered twins, but for some reason had rejected this one. The owner was a friend of my dad who did not have time to bottle feed it and offered it to us. Of course, we loved the lamb, who I promptly named Tinkerbell, and we took turns caring for him. We put him in a big box in our back porch because he was much too little to leave in the barn by himself. I remember hearing the thumping of his tiny tail against the side of the box when we would take him a bottle. When he got a little bigger, I put a collar and leash on him and walked him around the yard like a puppy. He became my best little friend. Once he was mostly grown, we put him in the main pasture with our other animals. I remember one day going to visit him after school. I had been busy and not spent much time with him for a while. I wondered what his reaction would be – would he remember me? When I opened the gate and called his name, he came running! All it took was the sound of my voice calling his name. His joy was found in being by my side.

Do we recognize God's voice when he is calling us? Even if we haven't heard it for a long time? And if we recognize it, what do we do? Do we go running towards him, or do we continue what we are doing and ignore him? Or even walk in the other direction? Where do we find our joy?

Prayer: Dear Lord, I never want to be so busy and distracted that I do not hear and recognize your voice when you call. Help me to stay by your side, learning and growing from your teachings. And if I do wander away, help me to come running back to you. Amen

—

Application:

_____

_____

_____

_____

_____

_____

WEEK 19 – YOKE

Today's Scripture: Matthew 11:28-30
"Come to me, all you who are weary and burdened, and I will give you rest. Take my yoke upon you and learn from me, for I am gentle and humble in heart, and you will find rest for your souls. For my yoke is easy and my burden is light."

Reflection: As I mentioned before, my father grew up on a small farm in northern Minnesota. Long before there were gas-powered tractors, he worked his fields by hitching his horse to a small plow with a yoke (a wooden crossbeam attached across the neck of an animal with reins that the farmer would hold to guide the animal in the right direction.) My dad held the reins of the horse and the handles of the plow, and together they walked up and down the field, furrowing straight rows. The yoke was not used for punishment or to cause pain, but as a means for my dad to gently guide the horse and instruct him to start or stop, turn left or right. My dad used his skills as a farmer to keep the horse from wandering all over the field, making a mess of things and more work for everyone. He could guide the horse away from obstacles such as large rocks or trees, and the straight rows would lead to the best harvest possible. Many years later my dad brought that old plow to our new farm – not as an implement to be used in the field but as a reminder of all he had learned in his youth.

In our verses above, we see that God is calling us to put on his yoke and let him take the reins of our lives, guiding us in paths of righteousness. He knows what is best for us: when we need to move forward and when it is time to rest. As the horse trusted my dad to be gentle and kind, so we can trust the ultimate farmer who knows the best ways to go, even on our most difficult days

Prayer: Many times I am weary, but I usually find it is when I have tried to do things on my own. Help me to turn to you and submit my will to your yoke, realizing that your gentle guidance will lead me in paths of success and away from pain and harm. Thank you for teaching me your ways. Amen

Application:

_____

_____

_____

_____

_____

_____

WEEK 20 – FEED THE BIRDS

Today's Scripture: Matthew 6:26 "'Behold the fowls of the air: for they sow not, neither do they reap, nor gather into barns, yet your heavenly Father feedeth them. Are you not much better than they?"

Reflection: My mother loved birds and had many styles of birdfeeders and birdhouses. She would sit for hours watching the wrens dart back and forth building their nests and waited anxiously for the first hummingbirds each spring. But one thing was always very obvious – those birds were busy! Whether big or small, beautifully colored or plain, they worked from dawn until dusk to take care of their families. And they did all of that while sharing their songs with those around them. As my pastor once told me, "Yes, God does feed the birds. But He doesn't throw the worms up into the tree!" The same is true for us. God continues to provide blessings to us each day, but we need to do our part by getting up each morning and using our gifts and energy to serve our families and our communities. He provides the resources – the skills, talents, and opportunities – but it is up to us to do the work. And to do it cheerfully, with a song!

Prayer: Heavenly Father, thank you for all the gifts You freely give to me. Help me to see that your lavish provision of skills and talents is meant for my good and the good of the world around me. Let me always strive to stay joyfully busy in the works you have planned for me. Amen

Application:

_____

_____

_____

_____

_____

_____

WEEK 21 – DO NOT LEAVE ME

Today's Scripture: Psalm 38:21-22 "Lord, do not forsake me; do not be far from me, my God. Come quickly to help me, my Lord and my Savior."

Reflection: King David's life was filled with highs and lows. He experienced many successes on the battlefield, with victory over Goliath as a highlight. However, his life was often in danger as he was hunted down by a jealous King Saul and spent years in hiding. God had plans for his future, but they were hard to see when he was living in exile in the mountains. David felt alone and abandoned by the God he had committed to serve.

How easy it is for us to feel the same way — when our child is sick or injured and the doctors are not optimistic, when a friend or spouse has betrayed us, or when there has been the loss of a job or home due to circumstances out of our control. We cry out to God and wonder if He even hears us. Deuteronomy 31:6-8 states "Be strong and courageous. Do not fear or be in dread of them, for it is the LORD your God who goes with you. He will not leave you or forsake you." God is at work in ways we cannot always see and working for our good. There is a popular song "Trust His Heart" which contains these lines, "God is too wise to be mistaken, God is too good to be unkind. So when you don't understand, When you don't see His plan, When you can't trace His hand, Trust His Heart"

Prayer: Heavenly Father, please help us to remember that you are always with us, even if we do not immediately see or feel your presence. Help us to trust your promises to never leave or forsake us. We know that you love us and want only your best for us – help us to not be afraid but to see your hand at work around us. Amen

Application:

_____

_____

_____

_____

_____

_____

WEEK 22 – ETERNAL HOPE

Today's Scripture: Psalm 62:5-6 "Yes, my soul, find rest in God; my hope comes from him. Truly he is my rock and my salvation; he is my fortress; I will not be shaken."

Reflection: In early November of 2021, my mother was diagnosed with advanced pancreatic cancer. The disease spread rapidly, and she passed away February 17, 2022, just two months short of her 91st birthday. But despite excruciating pain and the loss of all ability to care for herself, she never once lost her faith in God, or her anticipation of an eternity spent with him.

During the last few days of her life, she faded in and out of the ability to speak and to understand what was said to her. Each of my siblings and most of her grandchildren were able to spend time with her, either in person or over the phone. But before she faded away completely, she raised her hands toward heaven and said, "I see HIM! I see all the forgiven ones!" She asked one of my nieces to sing with her, and my mother (who was NOT a singer) boldly (and on key!) sang "Blessed Assurance" and "The Doxology" with a clear, strong voice. Some of her last words were "Thank you Lord for welcoming me into your Kingdom," and "I'm ready to go home to Heaven." Her unwavering hope and faith were an example for all of us.

Hope for the future, a glorious future with him in heaven, even during the darkest shadows of death: That is what is available to all of us. As the famous old hymn states, "My hope is in the Lord, who gave himself for me, and paid the price of all my sin at Calvary. For me he died; for me he lives. And everlasting life and light he freely gives."

Prayer: Dear Heavenly father, thank you for the hope you give each of us: hope for comfort here on earth and hope for an eternity in your presence. Thank you for the lessons of hope we can learn from others. Amen

Application:

_____

_____

_____

_____

_____

_____

WEEK 23 – SHOW ME THE WAY

Today's Scripture: Psalm 143:8 "Let the morning bring me word of your unfailing love, for I have put my trust in you. Show me the way I should go, for to you I entrust my life."

Reflection: Our alarm goes off and we wearily open our eyes to face another day. What is our attitude as we stretch and yawn? We can either smile and say, "Good morning, Lord!" or grumble and mumble "Good Lord, morning?" Our initial thoughts can play a big part in our actions and interactions during the day. Some people stumble into the kitchen for a steaming cup of coffee, others headfirst to the shower. I keep a small journal next to my bed where I have promises listed along with a brief morning prayer to aid in reminding me of God's faithfulness and His willingness to help me throughout my day. I find peace not by scrolling through social media or watching the morning news but by starting my day in quiet reflection and praise. These practices help me focus on Him as challenges arise during the day.

Prayer: Thank you, Lord, for another night of rest, and for waking me this morning. Great is your faithfulness to me. Thank you for the many blessings you have so freely given to me. Go with me today as I meet others at work or at play. Guide my conversations and my footsteps as I seek to be your hands, feet, and voice in the world today. Amen

Application:

_____

_____

_____

_____

_____

_____

WEEK 24 – ORANGE JUICE

Today's Scripture: 2 Timothy 1:6 "Wherefore I put thee in remembrance that thou stir up the gift of God, which is in thee."

Reflection: I love orange juice, especially juice with lots of pulp. To me, it's almost like eating an actual orange. But have you ever poured yourself a big glass only to find that the pulp had all settled to the bottom of the carton? What comes out first is just thin juice with none of the rich goodness. This watered-down liquid is not appealing, but neither is the thickness left on the bottom of the container. The only way to ensure that you get a glass that is a nice mixture of juice and pulp is to shake it up first. So it can be with you and me. Sometimes our faith has been inactive and 'on the shelf' for so long that the fullness of our testimony has become sluggish. When a crisis happens, unfortunately what flows out of our hearts is a pale version of our ability to recall scripture or to experience God's peace through His promises. Only by keeping our faith well-stirred by frequent prayer and Bible study are we able to respond to life's challenges with complete trust and confidence as God intended.

Prayer: Lord of all blessings and truth, I don't want an inactive faith that has been tucked carefully on the shelf but of no real appeal or value. Keep my heart and soul stirred with your truths through Bible study and prayer. Flood my mind with wholesome entertainment and activities. Keep my testimony fresh and vibrant, appealing to others, so that I can draw them to you. Amen

Application:

_____

_____

_____

_____

_____

_____

WEEK 25 – YOU ARE RADIANT

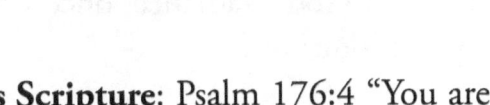

Today's Scripture: Psalm 176:4 "You are radiant with light, more majestic than mountains rich with game."

Reflection: I have always loved nature and many times my mom would find me sitting quietly in the woods on our farm or alongside the creek listening to the animals, the babble of the water, and the soft breeze in the trees. I would often get up early to observe a glorious sunrise and watch the world come to life. I had my own pony, and I would frequently ride to the far pasture and just sit silently to look at the clouds or listen to the birds singing their songs to each other. One summer we packed our camper and headed to the Black Hills, and I remember Dad stopping the car and we were all amazed as we saw the hundreds of bison that dotted the hillsides for as far as we could see. Another vacation took us to Colorado, and I fell in love with the grandeur of God's handiwork – the immense mountains jutting up into the sky. How amazing it is to think that no matter the beauty that we see here on earth, it is but a fraction of the majesty that awaits us in heaven. The awe-inspiring colors of an early morning sunrise will be but a pale reflection of God's radiance, once we are in the presence of our Lord.

Prayer: Dear Lord, creator of everything beautiful, I thank you for all the splendor that surrounds us each day, if we will but look. But more than that, I thank you for the majesty that awaits us once we join you in heaven. While we can only imagine what it will be like, I thank you for giving us a small glimpse of that now.

Application:

_____

_____

_____

_____

_____

_____

WEEK 26 – SHADOWS

Today's Scripture: Psalm 23:4 "Yea, though I walk through the valley of the shadow of death, I will fear no evil; for thou art with me; thy rod and thy staff they comfort me."

Reflection: When I was young, my family visited a cave that had a boat ride as part of the experience. I remember straining to see the water from our pontoon as shadows flickered on the walls from a few dimly lit candles. I remember being nervous. But then our tour guide turned off all the lights! The entire cave was plunged into complete darkness – I could not see my hands or my brother sitting next to me. I was afraid to move for fear of falling into the black water. There were no more shadows, just an overpowering wall of …. nothingness. Even though I knew there were other people nearby, I felt very alone. After what seemed an eternity (but was probably just a few seconds) the lights were turned back on. What a relief! Even the presence of just a small bit of light was such a comfort! But God is our true source of light, and how much more comfort we can have knowing that he is with us during our difficult times. Just as in the cave where there were no shadows without a source of light, we can pass through life's shadows, even the shadow of death, knowing that God is providing His light to guide us.

Prayer: Dear God, our ever-present source of light and comfort: help me to recognize that you are beside me during the challenging times of my life. Even though fear and shadows gather around me, remind me of Your presence and guidance. You have not left me alone in the darkness but provide light and the comfort of your love. Amen

Application:

_____

_____

_____

_____

_____

_____

WEEK 27 – FORGIVENESS

Today's Scripture: Matthew 18:21-22 "Then Peter came and said to Him, "Lord, how often shall my brother sin against me and I forgive him? Up to seven times?" Jesus said to him, "I do not say to you, up to seven times, but up to seventy times seven.""

Reflection: I'm not an athletic person – never have been, never will be. I went to a VERY small high school where the only cool kids were the athletes. I was mercilessly teased for years about my lack of abilities, and the fact that I was always the last one to be picked for a team in PE. Other talents such as music or a high IQ meant nothing to this group, and I harbored resentment for years. Just a few years ago I was at a reunion and was introduced to the new wife of a former classmate. As we were getting to know each other, she asked if I ever participated in sports in school. On the other side of the table was one of my biggest tormenters, who rolled her eyes and made a hideous face. Instantly, I felt like I was 13 again with the old insecurities rushing back. I told my new friend that no, I did not play sports but found other ways to support my school by being in the pep band and playing at all the games. Then I looked back at my tormenter and realized that I was not mad anymore, and actually just felt pity for her that she still carried such resentment. My forgiveness towards her lifted a giant weight from my shoulders.

Prayer: Lord, please develop in me a more forgiving spirit. Help me to realize that harboring resentment is only hurting me, and that I am to forgive others just as you have forgiven me. Help me not to judge the motive of others through my earthly eyes but through your heavenly heart. Amen

Application:

_____

_____

_____

_____

_____

_____

WEEK 28 – PERFECTION

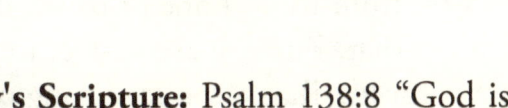

Today's Scripture: Psalm 138:8 "God is at work in my life, and He will perfect everything that concerns me."

Reflection: Perfection – what a scary word. Perfection at school, perfection in our homes, perfection at work, perfection in our relationships, perfection at church. It's all too much sometimes. I remember spending hours and hours studying for a test and getting a 104 out of 105. The comments from friends and some family members were "That's nice, but which one did you miss?" Except for an occasional Olympic athlete, I'm not sure any of us will achieve perfection while here on earth. But where does all the pressure come from, and the feeling of low self-worth if we do not achieve it? And who are we allowing to set the standards, to determine our success? And why are we allowing it to stress us so?

I'm so thankful that God is perfect, and that He is working on my behalf. Will life be perfect?

Of course not. But His love for us is, and that's all that really matters.

Prayer: Thank you, Lord, that you do not expect perfection from us, as none of us would be able to achieve that. But you are perfect in your love and care for us. Thank you for loving us. Amen

Application:

_____

_____

_____

_____

_____

_____

WEEK 29 – REFRESH

Today's Scripture: Jeremiah 31:25 "I will refresh the weary and satisfy the faint."

Reflection: Have you ever been so tired that you did not think you could take another step? So exhausted that you could not go on? A few years ago, I found myself needing to move from one apartment to another in the middle of the summer. I was trying to save money by moving most of the small things myself. Trip after trip, box after box, I pushed myself to try to accomplish as much as possible before the movers came for the furniture and big items. That evening I packed my swollen knees in ice and prayed for endurance. I just didn't know how I was going to do everything myself. Shortly before I went to bed, I got a call from a friend at church who offered to come over and help me. The next day she brought a flatbed trailer and about 10 helpers. I'm not quite sure how she knew I needed help, but it was so appreciated! They insisted that I remain seated at my old apartment and then had me sit at the new place as well. My friends made short work of what would have taken me hours.

How much more does God want to help us during our difficult days – whether physically, mentally, or emotionally. Rest in him – let him be the one to restore your weary body or mind.

Prayer: Dear Father, thank you for the refreshment you give to my weary soul. Life is hard and I am often faced with situations too difficult to handle alone. Thank you that you can provide answers, even before I ask. Amen

Application:

_____

_____

_____

_____

_____

_____

WEEK 30 – PRECIOUS THOUGHTS

Today's Scripture: Psalm 139:17-18 "How precious are your thoughts about me, O God. They cannot be numbered! They outnumber the grains of sand! And when I wake up, you are still with me."

Reflection: Do you remember the first time you fell in love? Whether as a teenager or a young adult, thoughts of this special person occupied your thoughts and actions. You would wait anxiously for a letter to come in the mail or the phone to ring, or in today's world, the arrival of a text message or video chat. We could talk for hours with this person, barely sleeping or eating, and counting the minutes until we could be together again. We read their letters over and over again - we could not imagine our lives without this person by our side.

It's amazing to think that God loved us before we even knew about him, and that he thinks about each of us constantly. He has already written his love letter to us – how anxious are we to read it? He reaches out to us daily through his Spirit, and through the words and guidance of others. Do we recognize his voice? Do we respond back to him with loving thoughts of our own?

Prayer: Dear Heavenly Father - I cannot fathom the love you have for me, and for each of us. Thank you for your Word which tells me how much you care. Help me to respond to your love and to share that love with others. Amen

Application:

_____

_____

_____

_____

_____

_____

WEEK 31 – ANXIETY

Today's Scripture: Proverbs 12:23 "Anxiety weights down the heart, but a kind word cheers it up."

Reflection: There are many times when it is perfectly normal to feel anxious – starting a new school or job, moving to a new city, learning some discouraging health news, having more month than paycheck. All of us struggle at times, and it's easy to feel isolated and alone with our fears.

But our verse today tells us to be kind to one another. A gentle word, a smile, and showing interest in another person's situation can work wonders to ease their anxiety. But in order to do this we need to really SEE the other person and recognize their struggles. Perhaps that means putting down our cell phones when we are with other people or turning off the TV or gaming system. Maybe it means asking gentle questions and offering a sympathetic ear without judgment.

A tender show of concern could mean the world to them. But what if WE are the one struggling? There is no shame in asking for help. Taking our anxieties to God in prayer is the best solution, as he will always express his love and concern for us. As I Peter 5:7 tells us, "Casting all your care upon him; for he careth for you."

Prayer: Dear Father, help me to be more aware of those who are struggling and to reach out to them during their time of anxiety. And when I am feeling anxious, help me remember to bring my concerns to you. Amen

Application:

_____

_____

_____

_____

_____

_____

WEEK 32 – TEACH ME

Today's Scripture: Romans 15:4 "And the scriptures were written to teach and encourage us by giving us hope"

Reflection: I have always loved going to school. From the first day of kindergarten when I was too short to climb on the bus unassisted to several college experiences, school has always excited me. I was a good student (even if I did get in trouble for talking too much) and I remember crying on the last day of third grade because I was going to miss my teacher and my friends. Little did I know that in just a few months I would meet a woman who would have a huge impact on my life. Mrs. T was an amazing teacher and inspired in me an even deeper love of reading and writing. She took an interest in each one of us individually, and I worked hard to always do my best for her. She taught me how to research topics for essays and how to problem-solve on my own. She encouraged me to spread my wings and to be willing to try new things. We stayed in touch even after I graduated, and I counted her as a dear friend.

What made me successful in her class, however, was my willingness to learn. Our verse today tells us that the scriptures were written to teach us, but we must ask ourselves these questions: do I want to learn what God is wanting to teach me? Sometimes the lessons are hard, or inconvenient, or costly. Am I willing to do the work to study and research? To listen to those more knowledgeable than me as they explain complicated topics? When was the last time I actually sat down and read my Bible, let alone study its teachings? God's word is filled with hope, but I need to open the covers and let him teach me.

Prayer: Dear God – thank you for earthly teachers who inspire in us a love for learning. They often go unappreciated, and I ask that you bless them for their contributions. And thank you, also, for your word which is available to me in a multitude of translations and electronic forms. Help me to be willing to study your word and learn what lessons you have for me. Amen

Application:

_____

_____

_____

_____

_____

_____

WEEK 33 – GUILT

Today's Scripture: Psalm 85:2 "You took away your people's guilt; you covered all their sin."

Reflection: When I was in college, I woke up one Sunday morning to find there had been a light dusting of snow that was covering the grass and trees, and my car of course. As someone who had grown up in the Midwest, shoveling and scraping snow was nothing new, but was certainly not my favorite thing to do. After cleaning my car, I drove to the local church I was attending while in school. Near the parking lot was a huge tree that had been damaged in a storm the past summer. There were broken and missing branches and its contorted form was an ugly contrast to what it used to be. However, on this morning all the scars were covered by the snow, and once the sun came out, it glistened like it was covered with diamonds. The reflection was so bright I could barely look at it. All the hurt and damage was hidden from view.

How thankful I am that God's love covers the ugly parts of my life once I have asked for forgiveness. He doesn't look at me as damaged or defective - I can stand sparkling and pure before Him, not as someone filled with guilt and shame. But although snow melts and physical hurts reappear, I trust that I can be covered daily by his love that washes me so I can be whiter than snow.

Prayer: Dear Father – thank you that your love covers my sins, and that I can stand before you unafraid. I have no power to cover my sin and guilt, but your love erases them all and I am pure and clean in your sight. Help me to walk worthy of this amazing gift. Amen

Application:

_____

_____

_____

_____

_____

_____

WEEK 34 – WORK

Today's Scripture: Colossians 3:23 "Work willingly at whatever you do, as though you were working for the Lord rather than for people."

Reflection: My siblings and I were not always the most obedient children. On Saturdays, our father was often at work and our mother would go to town for a few hours to run some errands and get groceries. She would leave a list of things she wanted us to do around the house before she got back. Each of us was assigned to a particular duty such as vacuuming the living room or cleaning the kitchen. But it did not take us many weeks to learn that we could put off our chores for at least an hour and still have them done before Mom got home. In fact, we could actually see her car while it was still far away, and it took some time for her to drive down the long driveway and start to unload the groceries. We invented a game called "Mom's coming down the driveway!" and once one of us spotted her car, we would rush frantically around and clean, and then pretend to be relaxing once she came in the house. Of course, spending just one or two minutes cleaning the bathroom was certainly not doing a good job of it, especially since it was the only bathroom for seven people! But we thought we were being very clever pulling the wool over mom's eyes. Yes, the chores got done but we certainly did not use our best efforts. Mom never did complain, and I think secretly she admired our creativity.

As I got older, however, I could not help but feel a bit guilty. We worked hard when she was present but then slacked off when she was away. I was not living true to what she had been teaching about hard work and integrity. Eventually we confessed, and all got a good laugh about it. But we are to respect those in authority and to work hard, even if they are not around to see our efforts. We are diligent in our work for the Lord; we should be the same in our work for others.

Prayer: Father, it is so easy for me to not do my best in my work when no one is watching. Help me to remember to respect those in authority, and to do my work as if it was being given to you. Because in reality, all that I do is for you.

Even if no one knows that I am slacking in my work, you do. Thank you for the reminder to be conscientious in all that I do. Amen

Application:

_____

_____

_____

_____

_____

_____

WEEK 35 – SLOW TO ANGER

Today's Scripture: James 1:19 "Be quick to listen, slow to speak, and slow to anger."

Reflection: Angry words spoken in haste can leave wounds that are very difficult to heal. A teacher once had her class take a piece of plain paper and wad it up into a ball. The students were to stomp on it, smash it, maybe even tear the edges a bit. Then they were asked to unfold the paper and try to smooth it back into its original form. Of course, they could not as the damage to the papers was too significant. She then explained that those wrinkles represented harshly spoken words of anger or bullying. Even if the offender later apologized, the harm was done, and the scars would remain. I was on the receiving end of one particularly hurtful exchange with someone I respected. Without knowing all the facts or taking the time to hear my side of the story, they lashed out in anger and disappointment. Years later an apology was made, but how much better it would have been if they could have been a bit slower in their response.

James is instructing us here to spend our time listening first before reacting. Perhaps if we spend more time listening than speaking, we can avoid doing damage to those around us.

Prayer: Dear Father - Please guide my thoughts and actions during times of confrontation. Help me not to lash out too quickly before I know all the facts. Remind me to listen first before I respond. Amen

Application:

_____
_____
_____
_____
_____
_____

WEEK 36 – STUDY

Today's Scripture: 1 Peter 3:15 "If someone asks about your hope as a believer, always be ready to explain it."

Reflection: The score was tied at 80 for each team, with just one question left. My two sisters and a friend were on one side of the church and their biggest rival was just across the platform. The regional championship was on the line. The quizmaster said, "Question number 20, question: Quote Matthew 7:7." All six quizzers jumped from their seats. My oldest sister was the first one up and she quoted the verse correctly! The church erupted in applause as our team was awarded the trophy. Bible quizzing was a huge part of my upbringing – watching my older siblings when they were teens, and then having my turn a few years later. Hundreds of hours of studying and memorizing took place long before the first contests. Practice, teamwork, strategy…. all were parts of the process. Winning trophies was fun, but the main thing we all gained was learning God's word so thoroughly that we could recall it more than 50 years later and apply it to our lives now. I still remember verses I learned from Galatians, Ephesians and Philippians that I can use to help me with the issues and struggles of today. My younger brother has continued to be involved in quizzing and has coached for many years, even winning national championships. But what he stresses more than anything to his quizzers is to be able to apply the scripture to their lives.

Our verse for today tells us that we should be able to explain the hope we feel as believers. The best way to do that is to know and understand God's word. Memorization can be difficult at times but is such a comfort when God is able to bring a particular passage back to us just when we need it most.

Prayer: Dear Father – help me to want to not only read your word, but to study and memorize so that it is always fresh in my thoughts. Bring these verses back to me when I need them most – whether in times of trial or when I am asked about my faith. Amen

Application:

_____

_____

_____

_____

_____

_____

WEEK 37 – HARVEST

Today's Scripture: Galatians 6:9 "Let us not lose heart in doing good, for in due time we will reap if we do not grow weary."

Reflection: For my entire life leading up to when I left for college, my parents had a big garden. They both worked fulltime jobs (my dad often worked 2 or 3 jobs at a time) but there was always the concern with how to care for our large family. The plan for the garden was not just to feed us fresh foods during the summer but to be able to preserve enough to last throughout the coming winter. Mom's goal was to never have to buy vegetables at the store, although she would add lettuce or other greens occasionally. But to accomplish this, that meant the garden had to be tilled and planted with enough crops to freeze or preserve hundreds of quarts of corn, green beans, tomatoes, beet pickles and anything else she could find. But long before we were able to enjoy this bounty in the middle of winter, many hours of work had to be done first. Weeding, watering, thinning, even occasionally applying bug sprays, all were necessary weeks ahead of the harvest. Daily attention to the crops was needed. Then it was time for them to be picked, washed, and prepared for mom to spend endless hours with her pressure cooker or freezer containers, using jars or boxes that had been sterilized and made ready. I remember one summer when my younger brother and I spent an entire day husking corn for mom to freeze. We got tired and cranky, and even a little bit silly, and were thrilled when our part of the job was done around 3 pm. We went off to watch tv or take a nap while our mother remained in the kitchen for several more hours finishing up the 100 quarts of corn that she was able to put into our large chest freezer. At any time along the way my parents could have decided that there was just too much work involved in this whole process, but they never did. Caring for us was their primary objective.

How often do we get tired of doing good things when the harvest seems so far away? Endless hours of preparing Sunday School lessons, tutoring a struggling student where we volunteer, working in the nursery, taking meals to the sick – how easy it would be to just give up and let someone else do the work and worry about the results. But God has called each of us to be workers, and to continue that work until the harvest is done.

Prayer: Oh Lord, help me to keep going when I'm tired and the harvest seems so far away. I see the seed packets at the store and instantly want gorgeous beans or cucumbers. Help me when the days are long and hot to keep watering and weeding, so that when the day of harvest comes, my crops are ready and without blemish. Amen

Application:

_____

_____

_____

_____

_____

_____

WEEK 38 – WALKING IN STEP

Today's Scripture: Galatians 5:23 "Since we live by the Spirit, let us keep in step with the Spirit."

Reflection: From a young age I have always loved parades, especially the marching bands. It amazed me that the members could march in straight lines and play music at the same time. Keeping in perfect step, making intricate formations – it involved a huge amount of skill and teamwork. I was excited to be in our school band when I got older. Our band director had a love for parade marching, so many of our weekends were spent traveling to nearby towns and participating in festivals and holiday celebrations. The thing that made us successful as a band was how well we stayed in formation. We were acutely aware of keeping in line, not just on the straight roads but on curves and when turning corners. During band practice each day we would go outside and march on a side street, turning corners one after another. He wanted it to be second nature for us when we got to the next parade, so we could look confident in front of the crowds or judges if we were at a competition. And he was right – the more we practiced, the better we got.

Walking in faith is much the same way. Being part of God's family means walking daily with the Spirit as my guide. Keeping in step with him will help me when life throws curves at me, or I find it is time to turn a corner. I'm certainly not perfect, but with daily practice I am becoming more confident as I go down the road of life.

Prayer: Dear Lord, keep me close to you, and in step with you. Guide me during the straight times of life as well as the difficult curves. Amen

Application:

_____

_____

_____

_____

_____

_____

WEEK 39 – WWJD

Today's Scripture: Psalm 119:11 "I have hidden your word in my heart, that I might not sin against you."

Reflection: WWJD. What Would Jesus Do. This phrase became popular several years ago, and soon was plastered on t-shirts, jewelry, billboards and just about everywhere else. The idea was that we were to stop before acting or saying something rude and ask ourselves what Jesus would do under these same circumstances. But how are we to know what Jesus would do if we have not read the instruction book he wrote for us? Or if we have not memorized his teachings?

When I was in college, I was one of those strange students who loved writing term papers. Researching, taking notes on hundreds of notecards, making outlines – I loved it all. In my American History class, we were assigned to write a paper about post-Civil War reconstruction. I glanced at the syllabus and thought I understood the requirements. Many hours were spent in the library, and I read any book I could find on the subject. I formulated my ideas and started writing – fully anticipating being done early so I had time to review and revise if needed. We had the entire semester to work on it, but I was excited to be so far ahead of everyone. A few weeks before the paper was due, I was chatting with one of my classmates who said he was struggling with the assignment, since it was to be written as if President Lincoln had NOT been assassinated – um, what? Not assassinated? Where did that come from? I played along with him, but inside was panicking. I could not wait to get home and look at the syllabus – and yes, there it was in plain sight. The paper was to be written as if Lincoln was alive! I'm glad I found out then before I turned the paper in, but now I only had a few weeks to re-write my paper, instead of several months. In my haste to jump in and get started, I had neglected to read all the instructions.

God has given us the ultimate syllabus for our lives, but it is up to us to read and understand it. When we are faced with decisions, we should either know the answers or know where to find them.

Prayer: Dear Heavenly Father – thank you for the instructions you have given us so we can make the best decisions for our lives. Help us to not rush through those instructions, but to read them carefully so we can be confident to always know the best path to take. Amen

Application:

_____

_____

_____

_____

_____

_____

WEEK 40 – HAPPY BIRTHDAY

Today's Scripture: Proverbs 9:11 "For by me your days will be multiplied, and years of life will be added to you."

Reflection: Birthdays were always a fairly big deal in my family. While there was not a lot of money for parties or expensive gifts, we were made to feel special on our special day. Mom would let us decide what kind of cake we wanted (mine was usually orange with orange frosting) and what to have for dinner, within reason of course. We sang, blew out candles, and the birthday person was the center of attention, at least for a little while. One year my younger brother got two cool firetrucks AND a xylophone, which the rest of us were a bit jealous about. But our parents did their best to focus on us and provide what they could.

Our scripture tells us that it is God who numbers our days and adds just the right amount to our lives. We have no idea when we celebrate this year if there will be 10 more birthdays in the future, or 20, or only two. What we do know, however, is that we are to live each year with love, life, and laughter. Try not to focus on the gift you did not receive (or be jealous of someone else's gifts) but learn to take each day as a gift from God to be used for his glory.

Prayer: Dear Father, thank you for birthdays. Thank you that you know the day we arrived and the day we are to leave to be with you in heaven. Help us to make the most of our time here on earth. Amen

Application:

_____

_____

_____

_____

_____

_____

WEEK 41 – SPEAK CLEARLY

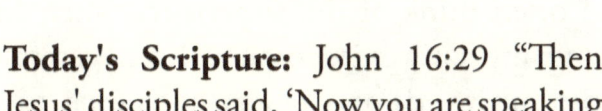

Today's Scripture: John 16:29 "Then Jesus' disciples said, 'Now you are speaking clearly and without figures of speech."

Reflection: Many years ago, I attended a very large church on the east coast. The number of people in my Sunday School class was more than the total attendance of most of the churches in my past. It is the first church I have ever attended that had an interpreter for their deaf ministry. I loved watching the interpreter and learned a fair amount of sign language from her. One Sunday the pastor was preaching and using a word I had never heard before. I've been in church all my life and consider myself to be fairly comfortable with Bible terminology, but this one word had me stumped. And judging by the confused faces of those sitting around me, I was not the only one. I happened to be sitting near the interpreter who seemed to be having a bit of trouble with this word as well, and had to finger-spell it each time. Finally in her frustration, she used a sign that I was familiar with and suddenly the whole message made sense! But to those who could not read sign language, the message was probably a waste of time.

I often think of this experience when I am sharing my faith with others. I am careful to choose my words and tailor my speech to the person I am speaking to. Until I get to know someone, I have no idea of their faith history or knowledge of the Bible. We cannot assume that the person we are talking to is as familiar with scripture as we are, or even has a Bible. We need to meet others where they are and not use big words just to show that we know them.

Prayer: Dear Father – Help me to be observant and to use words that are appropriate to the person I am speaking to. I know there others who have more Bible education than I do, and many who have much less. Help me to use clear examples and to listen for levels of understanding. Amen

Application:

_____

_____

_____

_____

_____

_____

WEEK 42 – SECURITY

Today's Scripture: Psalm 122:7 "May there be peace within your walls and security within your palaces."

Reflection: When I first went away to college, I lived in an apartment with three other girls I had never met before. It was a one-bedroom apartment with two sets of bunk beds and one bathroom. Suddenly I was living extremely close with total strangers, and it took quite some time for us to adjust to each other. After one particularly grueling day of tests and homework, I came back to our apartment completely exhausted. All I wanted was to turn on some quiet music and take a nap. What I found when I opened the door, however, was that two of my roommates had decided to throw a party – a very rowdy party with multiple illegal substances. The music was blaring, and our small apartment was packed with at least 20 people, most of whom did not go to our school. I went into the bedroom to change and put away my things, only to find someone already in my bed. I ended up going out to the parking lot and sleeping in the back seat of my car. So much for my peaceful nap!

God wants us to have safe and peaceful homes and to feel secure in our surroundings. I knew this was not the way I wanted to experience college. After a few phone calls and talks with my advisor, I was able to move into a different apartment with people who were more closely aligned with my values. Don't be afraid to ask God for help with anything, especially if you feel your safety has been compromised.

Prayer: Dear God – thank you for keeping me safe that day, and the days that followed. Help me to trust you to provide the things I need, including peaceful places to live. Amen

Application:

_____

_____

_____

_____

_____

_____

WEEK 43 – WORKMANSHIP

Today's Scripture: Ephesians 2:10 "For we are his workmanship, created in Christ Jesus for good works."

Reflection: One year I had the opportunity to visit a town that was famous for their crafts. We toured the woolen mills, the clock shop and the furniture factory. I watched as a plain piece of wood went entirely through the process of becoming a table leg. Each craftsman took care that their part of the process was completed to perfection. If a mistake was made, the process was stopped and then started again with a fresh piece of wood. The defective piece was put aside to be used for some lesser project. I was in awe as I watched each step in the process, and the furniture was exquisite when finished. I remember wanting to buy something to take home, but that level of craftsmanship came with a hefty price.

God created each of us with care and an attention to detail. He watched over us as we were formed in our mother's bodies and designed us to be unique and special. We are not leftovers or seconds, but perfection every time. How much more valuable are we to him than a table leg or a woolen scarf. And the price he paid for us was the life of his own son.

Prayer: Dear Lord – it amazes me to think that you made each of us exactly the way you wanted. We are precious and valuable to you – so valuable that Jesus died to bring us eternal life with you. Help me to never forget your love for me. Amen

Application:

_____

_____

_____

_____

_____

_____

WEEK 44 – THANKSGIVING

Today's Scripture: Psalm 107:8-9 "Let them give thanks to the Lord for his unfailing love and his wonderful deeds for mankind, for he satisfies the thirsty and fills the hungry with good things."

Reflection: Thanksgiving was always a special time for my family when I was growing up and continued that way as I became an adult. No matter where we gathered, there was always an abundance of our favorite foods, fun and laughter. My mother began planning weeks in advance and started stocking up on the items she knew she would need. She especially loved baking pies and made sure we each got the kind we wanted: blueberry for my older brother, pumpkin for my younger brother, lemon meringue for me, cherry for dad, and apple for my daughter, along with a variety of others. All my life my mom loved baking pies, and she tried numerous times to teach me. I failed to learn but my daughter did, and each year she would spend a whole day with her grandmother making pies. I never did quite understand how mom managed to cook such an enormous amount of food and have it all ready at the same time. It always looked and smelled amazing. But before any of us could start to eat, we would stand in a giant circle and hold hands. I would look around the room and thank God for my ever-growing family who took this special day to gather together. Dad would then give thanks for the food, for each one of us and for the blessings we had received that year. His prayer always seemed to reach straight to heaven. I am so thankful for these wonderful memories with my family.

Prayer: Lord, help me to be aware of our blessings each day, not just on a special day set aside for it. Your blessings are new every morning! Amen

Application:

_____

_____

_____

_____

_____

_____

WEEK 45 – ONE BODY

Today's Scripture: I Corinthians 12:27 "All of you together are Christ's body and each of you is a part of it."

Reflection: Several years ago, I fell on the ice and severely injured my shoulder. I went to the ER and was put in a sling with instructions NOT to use my arm for four weeks. I'm left-handed, and this was my right arm, so I figured it would be no big deal. I was so wrong. I could not raise my arm to wash my hair, use the mouse on my computer or even shift my car from park to drive. Washing dishes, folding laundry, everything - what I figured would be just a minor inconvenience turned into a real disruption in my life. Even after I got out of the sling, my shoulder was very tender, and I had to do exercises to restore flexibility and strength.

God does not look at any of us as incidental or unnecessary but considers us all parts of his body. Whether the parts are big or small, easily seen or working quietly in the background, all the parts are important. Some may get more credit than others, but injury to any one of the parts causes the body to be in pain and not function properly.

Prayer: Dear Lord, help me to remember that I am an important part of your body here on earth. I have a part to play, and your work is incomplete without my contribution. Help me also to see the value in others I meet along the way. They may have different skills than I do, or come from a different background, but their value to the body cannot be ignored. Amen

Application:

_____

_____

_____

_____

_____

_____

WEEK 46 – EVERYTHING WE NEED

Today's Scripture: 2 Peter 1:3 "We have everything we need to live a life that pleases God."

Reflection: Shortly after the COVID-19 pandemic began, I started having my groceries delivered. It was so easy to go online and decide what I wanted and a few hours later, or maybe the next day, everything was delivered to my door. No hassles with parking or standing in line - it was wonderful. One week I decided I was in the mood to bake and wanted to make my favorite orange cookies. I used to make them with my mom when I was younger, and the memories filled my heart. I completed my shopping order, making sure I had flour, sugar, eggs, and of course an orange. I would be needing both the juice and the zest for the frosting. I added other things for my regular order and waited anxiously for the next morning when my items would be delivered. About an hour before I expected things to arrive, I received an email saying there was one item that was sold out and unavailable – my orange! The most important ingredient! The weather was cold and rainy, and the last thing I wanted to do was to go somewhere looking for just one orange! What a disappointment!

Today's verse reminds us that things are not out of stock and no special trips are needed to find what is missing so we can be 'good enough' to serve God – he takes us as we are then provides all we need. Are we lacking in faith, peace, or joy? All we need to do is ask and he will deliver.

Prayer: Dear Father – thank you that you have provided all I need to serve you. My gifts and talents, a heart of worship, service to others --- you give me just what I need. Help me to feel worthy of those gifts, and to seek out ways to use them. Amen

Application:

_____

_____

_____

_____

_____

_____

WEEK 47 – WISDOM

Today's Scripture: James 1:5 "If any of you lacks wisdom, you should ask God, who gives generously to all without finding fault, and it will be given to you."

Reflection: Much of my professional life has been spent training others to do what I do. Whether taking students fresh off the street and starting at the beginning, or helping seasoned employees advance their careers to higher levels, teaching others has brought great joy to my life. When you see the lights go on and they finally grasp a complex subject, or I get to celebrate with them when they successfully pass a difficult certification exam – that makes all the hard work worth it. But my one biggest frustration and pet peeve is when a student comes to me and says, "I know this is a stupid question, but………." STOP! If you honestly do not know the answer, then the question is not stupid. None of us was born knowing how to do everything, and I certainly did not succeed in my profession without many hours spent in school learning things I did not previously know. My students were no different. Everyone needs to learn.

So it is with our relationship with God. He does not expect us to know all the answers but wants us to feel unafraid to approach him with our concerns. There are no 'stupid questions' when we honestly seek his wisdom and knowledge. He is waiting with a storehouse of understanding and will give more than we can imagine if we but ask in faith.

Prayer: Dear Father – thank you for your willingness to teach me what I need to know, and that you do so willingly and freely. There is so much I do not understand about you and your plan for my life. Help me to come to you boldly with my questions. Amen

Application:

_____

_____

_____

_____

_____

_____

WEEK 48 – DEVOTION

Today's Scripture: Colossians 4:2 "Devote yourselves to prayer, being watchful and thankful."

Reflection: It is always interesting when we meet someone new and spend some time getting to know them. We find out what they do (or did) for a living, where they went to school, if they are married or have children or grandchildren. We may learn about the places they have travelled or famous people they have met. Before too long we will learn about what they are truly passionate about. Whether it is a movie series like Star Wars, Harry Potter books, the latest video games, hobbies, or a musician they follow across the country, it usually does not take a long time to learn where their true devotions lie. Even now when I meet someone new, the first things I share are my job, where I live, and about my family. Perhaps it is today's society that has impressed on us not to discuss religion, but does my devotion to God ever enter into my conversations?

We are instructed in today's verse to be devoted to prayer to God, expressing our thankfulness to Him for all he has done for us. I struggle in this area, with my prayer life at times being dry and little more than 'thank you for this food' before a meal. God wants a relationship with us and that involves reading his word and talking with him. Have real and honest conversations. Thank him for the good things and ask for help with the difficult. Listen as well as speak. Draw near to God, and he will draw near to you.

Prayer: Dear Father – help me to be more devoted to an open and honest prayer life with you. I want to set aside the things of this world that don't really matter and develop the habit of spending quality time with you – thanking you for your goodness and your love and seeking guidance in times of difficulty. Help me to show that devotion to others I meet throughout my day. Amen

Application:

_____

_____

_____

_____

_____

_____

WEEK 49 – SEARCH ME

Today's Scripture: Psalm 139:23 "Search me, God, and know my heart; test me and know my anxious thoughts."

Reflection: Many years of my working life were spent travelling for my job – for almost 10 years I was on 2-3 flights every week. Connecticut one week, California the next: I racked up an amazing number of frequent flyer miles! Because I flew so often, I was an expert traveler and glided through security without any ordeal. Or at least I did until 9/11 happened. Suddenly the entire world was faced with the need to protect millions of flyers each day. Overnight there were new rules: Take off your shoes and belt; Empty your pockets; Allow yourself to be patted down aggressively by total strangers – it was the price we paid for the privilege to fly. Each time the security alerts seemed to be more random, and everyone's frustration and anxiety continued to rise. One time it was a package of gum in my purse that set off the alarm – another time it was a small stapler I carried with me for my job. I had nothing to hide, so ultimately the searches were little more than a nuisance. But it never became a pleasant experience.

In today's verse, David is asking to be searched – he wanted God to find anything that was out of place or needed to be removed. Do we boldly approach God and ask for him to find any hidden resentment or jealousy or unforgiveness? Do we really want to give up those things? Or do we hope that we can glide by with our hidden sins kept out of sight?

Prayer: Dear Father – I want you to search my heart as you did David's. I want nothing hidden from you. Show me things I need to get rid of, and places where things are lacking. I come before you boldly, knowing you only want what is best for me. Help me to obey and follow your instructions for my life. Amen

Application:

_____

_____

_____

_____

_____

_____

WEEK 50 – DO NOT BE AFRAID

Today's Scripture: Luke 2:10 "But the angel said to them, 'Do not be afraid; for behold, I bring you good news of great joy which will be for all the people.'

Reflection: The world today is filled with many things that could cause us to be fearful – urgent health issues and pandemics, political unrest, rising inflation, violence, and drug use: any one of these things could fill us with uneasiness and insomnia. No age group is exempt from what is happening in the world today, and it would be easy for us to lose our joy while watching 24-hour cable news or scrolling social media.

When the angel appeared to the shepherds on the hillside that night, it is understandable that they would be afraid – I certainly would have been! But how wonderful that they were the first to hear the good news of Jesus' birth! This news was not first given to the important people in society, the ones that others had deemed worthy or special, but to the lowly second-class citizens. This good news of great joy was given to ordinary people as a sign that God's love was for each of us. This perfect love came to earth to cast out our fears about the future.

Prayer: Thank you Lord for sending your Son to earth for each of us, regardless of our status or riches. Drive away our uncertainty about the future and enter into our celebrations this Christmas season. Help us keep the focus on you. Amen

Application:

_____

_____

_____

_____

_____

_____

WEEK 51 – A NEW THING

Today's Scripture: Isaiah 43:18-19 "Remember not the former things, nor consider the things of old. Behold, I am doing a new thing; I will make a way in the wilderness and rivers in the desert."

Reflection: My car was loaded to the brim and my dad and I said goodbye to mom before leaving to drive halfway across the country. I was 20 years old and moving to the east coast to live with my oldest sister. Her husband was in the Army and had just been deployed to Germany, leaving her alone with her 6-month-old son Andy. I was unhappy with my job as a legal secretary, and this was the perfect opportunity for me to get out of a bad situation and start over. The trip would take about 20 hours and dad wanted to drive straight through. We had his favorite snacks (orange slices), and I had a few hundred dollars along with all my possessions in suitcases and a couple of boxes. The long drive gave dad and I many hours to talk, and I expressed my nervousness with starting a new life in a strange city so far from home. Even though I would be living with my sister for about a year until her husband came home, I would need to find a job and learn to drive in a huge city. I wasn't sure I was ready for that. Dad told me stories about times in his life when he moved to someplace new and started over – when he left his childhood home for the Air Force, when he moved his growing family from Minnesota to Iowa for a better job, and when he left the security of a union job to go into business for himself. All were huge risks, and he had a family to provide for. But during each change he felt God's presence and leadership, and while there were many challenges and difficulties, he felt God's guidance. He stressed that I needed to get involved in a church right away with people my age who were in similar circumstances. And he wanted me to stay true to the values and ethics he and mom had taught me. How many times those words have replayed in my head over the years.

Prayer: Dear God – just as my earthly father gave me advice and guidance during this challenging time in my life, how much more as my Heavenly Father do you want to provide love and care for me every day. Thank you for always being there for me and opening the doors that lead to a life of devotion to you. Amen

Application:

_____

_____

_____

_____

_____

_____

WEEK 52 – FUTURE

Today's Scripture: Psalm 16:5 "Lord, You are my portion and my cup of blessing; You hold my future."

Reflection: As we reach the end of this year, it is only natural to look ahead and think about what the next year will bring. Will there be sickness or health? Financial prosperity or difficulties? New life or the death of a loved one? Will I find happiness? Will I be loved? Most everyone will do some sort of reflection on the past year and express hope for the next. What are you hoping for next year?

How secure we should feel that it is God who holds our future – that it is not up to us to stress and worry about, but that we should trust where he guides us. As we look back on the last months, do we clearly see the times where he led us? Can we recall when he spoke his healing power over us? Did we feel his peace and love during the difficult times? If he provided for us in the past, how much more we should trust him for the days to come.

Prayer: Thank you. Sometimes, God, that is all I can say. Thank you for your love and protection this past year. Thank you for providing for me and sending special people into my life when I needed them. And thank you that you are planning a bright future ahead for me, a future filled with faith and service to others. Help me to recognize your blessings in the future. Amen

Application:

_____

_____

_____

_____

_____

_____

FINAL THOUGHTS

Thank you for spending these past 52 weeks with me as we reflected on God's love and provision for our lives. It has been my pleasure to share my memories and the teachings of my parents and others who shaped me. My prayer is that you found them enjoyable to read and relatable to situations in your own life.

It is also my hope that these short devotionals have helped start a habit of weekly Bible reading or have supplemented the other readings you already do. I hope you will find time to memorize the verses that mean the most to you – I'm so thankful for the times God gives a verse back to me just when I need it.

May God richly bless you in the years to come.

Betty Gossell